TOP WORSHIP SONGS
FOR GUITAR

ISBN 978-1-4950-6551-4

HAL•LEONARD®
CORPORATION

7777 W. BLUEMOUND RD. P.O. BOX 13819 MILWAUKEE, WI 53213

Visit Hal Leonard Online at
www.halleonard.com

CONTENTS

Amazing Grace
(My Chains Are Gone)

Words by John Newton
Traditional American Melody
Additional Words and Music by Chris Tomlin and Louie Giglio

Because He Lives, Amen

**Words and Music by William J. Gaither, Gloria Gaither, Daniel Carson,
Chris Tomlin, Ed Cash, Matt Maher and Jason Ingram**

Break Every Chain

Words and Music by Will Reagan

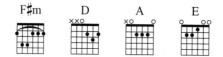

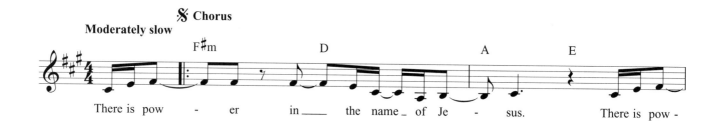

%. **Chorus**

Moderately slow

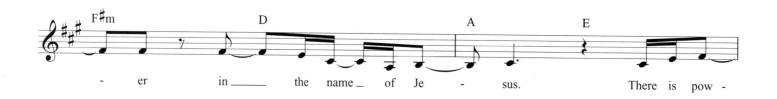

There is pow - er in ___ the name ___ of Je - sus. There is pow -

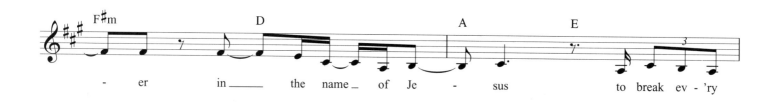

- er in ___ the name ___ of Je - sus. There is pow -

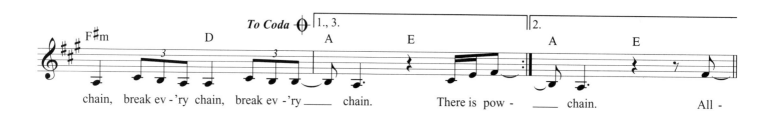

- er in ___ the name ___ of Je - sus to break ev - 'ry

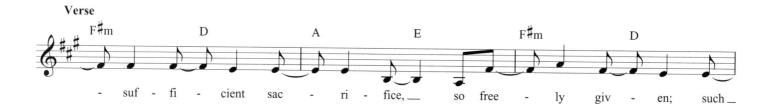

chain, break ev -'ry chain, break ev -'ry ___ chain. There is pow - ___ chain. All -

Verse

- suf - fi - cient sac - ri - fice, ___ so free - ly giv - en; such ___

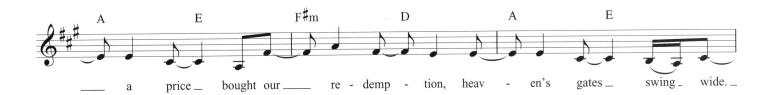

_____ a price _____ bought our _____ re - demp - tion, heav - en's gates _____ swing _____ wide. _____

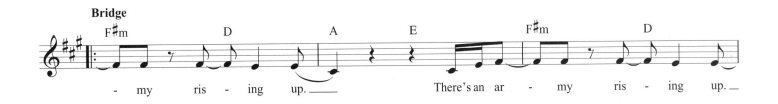

D.S. al Coda
(with repeat)

⊕ **Coda**

_____ There is pow - _____ chain. There's an ar -

Bridge

- my ris - ing up. _____ There's an ar - my ris - ing up. _____

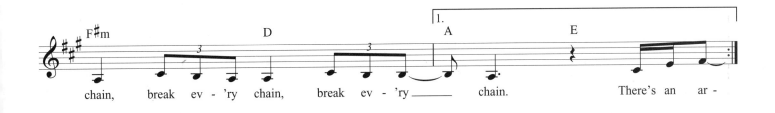

sing 8va 2nd time

_____ There's an ar - my ris - ing up _____ to break ev - 'ry

1.

chain, break ev - 'ry chain, break ev - 'ry _____ chain. There's an ar -

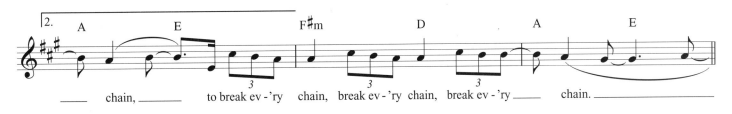

2.

_____ chain, _____ to break ev - 'ry chain, break ev - 'ry chain, break ev - 'ry _____ chain. _____

Interlude

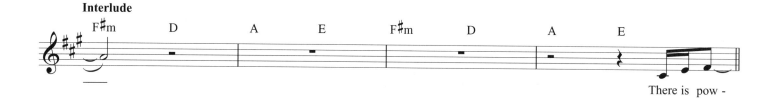

There is pow -

Chorus

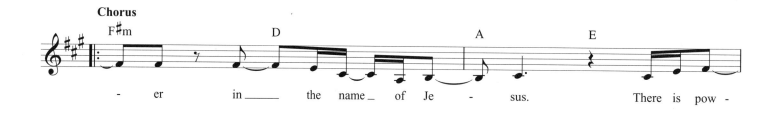

- er in _____ the name _ of Je - sus. There is pow -

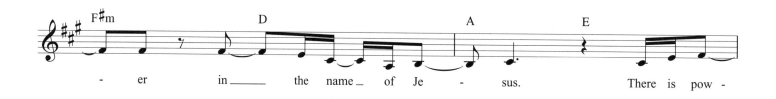

- er in _____ the name _ of Je - sus. There is pow -

sing 8va 2nd time

- er in _____ the name _ of Je - sus to break ev - 'ry

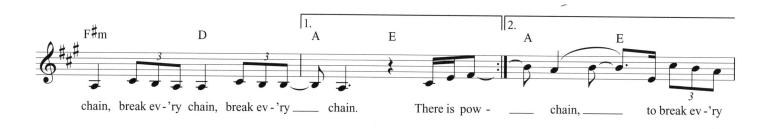

chain, break ev - 'ry chain, break ev - 'ry _____ chain. There is pow - _____ chain, _____ to break ev - 'ry

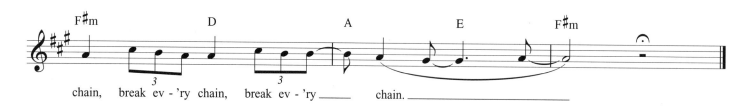

chain, break ev - 'ry chain, break ev - 'ry _____ chain. _____

Forever
(We Sing Hallelujah)

Words and Music by Brian Johnson, Christa Black Gifford,
Gabriel Wilson, Jenn Johnson, Joel Taylor and Kari Jobe

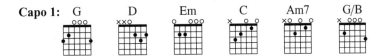

Capo 1: G   D   Em   C   Am7   G/B

Verse
Moderately

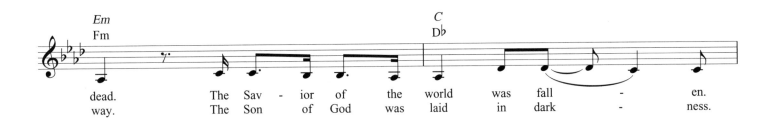

1. The moon and stars, they wept; the morn-ing sun was
2. One fi-nal breath He gave as heav-en looked a-

dead. The Sav-ior of the world was fall - en.
way. The Son of God was laid in dark - ness.

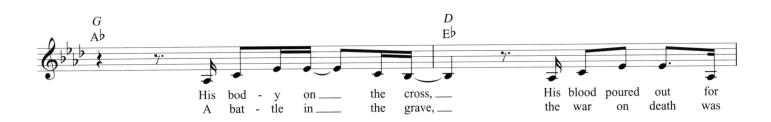

His bod-y on ___ the cross, ___ His blood poured out for
A bat-tle in ___ the grave, ___ the war on death was

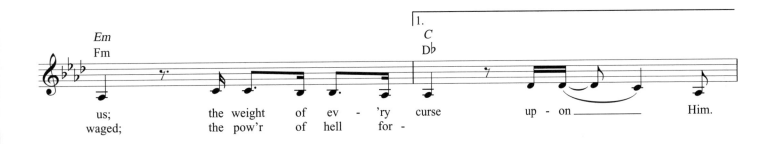

us; the weight of ev-'ry curse up-on _____ Him.
waged; the pow'r of hell for-

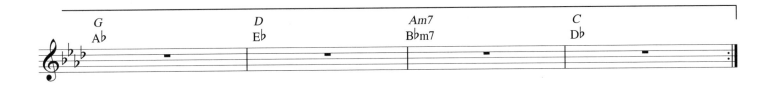

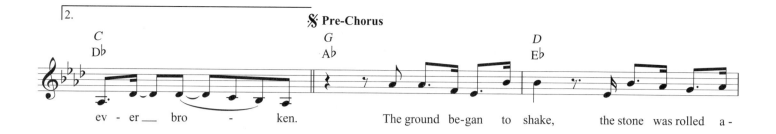

2.

C / Db — ev - er __ bro - ken.

§ Pre-Chorus

G / Ab — The ground be-gan to shake,

D / Eb — the stone was rolled a-

Em / Fm — way. His per - fect love __ could not be o - ver-come.

C / Db

G/B / Ab/C — Now, death, where __ is your __

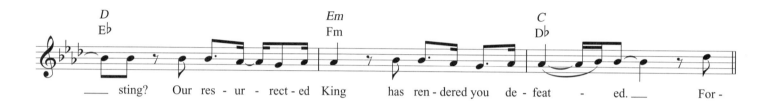

D / Eb — __ sting? Our res - ur - rect-ed King

Em / Fm — has ren - dered you de - feat - ed. __ For-

C / Db

Chorus

G / Ab — ev - er, He is glo - ri - fied.

D / Eb — For - ev - er, He is lift - ed high.

Em / Fm

C / Db — For-

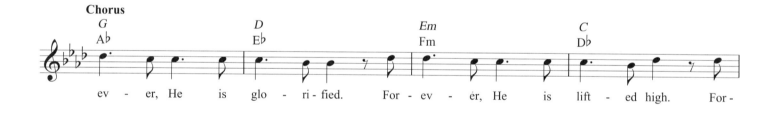

G / Ab — ev - er, He is ris - en.

D / Eb — He is a - live, __

To Coda ⊕

Em / Fm — He is a - live. __

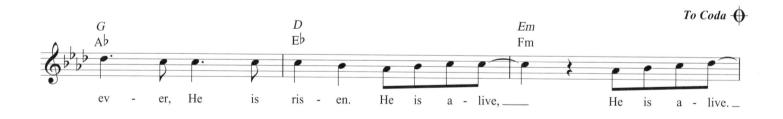

D.S. al Coda

C / Db — __

⊕ **Coda**

C / Db — __

Bridge

G / Ab — We sing hal - le - lu-

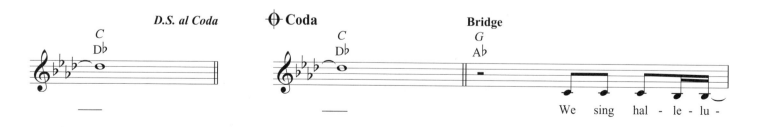

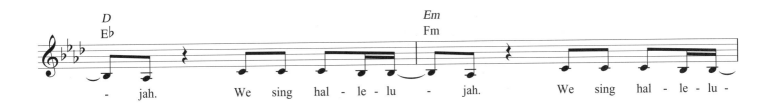

D
Eb

jah. We sing hal - le - lu - jah. Em / Fm *We sing hal - le - lu -*

C
Db

jah, the Lamb has o - ver - come. G / Ab *We sing hal - le - lu -*

D
Eb

jah. We sing hal - le - lu - jah. Am7 / Bbm7 *We sing hal - le - lu -*

Outro-Chorus

C
Db

jah, the Lamb has o - ver - come. G / Ab *For - ev - er, He is*

D / Eb   Em / Fm   C / Db   G / Ab

glo - ri - fied. For - ev - er, He is lift - ed high. For - ev - er, He is

D / Eb   Em / Fm   C / Db   G / Ab

ris - en. He is a - live, ___ He is a - live.

Broken Vessels
(Amazing Grace)

Words and Music by Joel Houston and Jonas Myrin

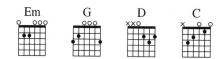

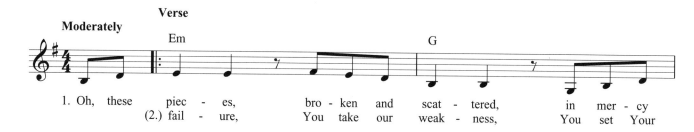

Verse

Moderately

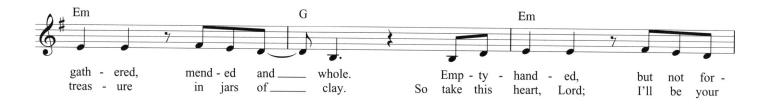

1. Oh, these piec - es, bro - ken and scat - tered, in mer - cy
(2.) fail - ure, You take our weak - ness, You set Your

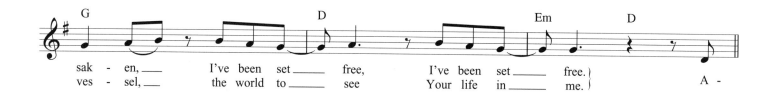

gath - ered, mend - ed and ___ whole. Emp - ty - hand - ed, but not for -
treas - ure in jars of ___ clay. So take this heart, Lord; I'll be your

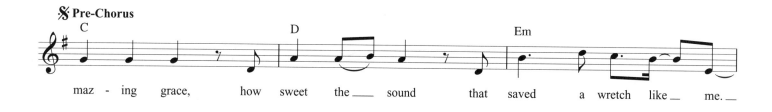

sak - en, ___ I've been set ___ free, I've been set ___ free.
ves - sel, ___ the world to ___ see Your life in ___ me. A -

Pre-Chorus

maz - ing grace, how sweet the ___ sound that saved a wretch like ___ me. ___

___ Ooh, whoa. ___ I once was lost, but now I am found; was

blind, but now I ___ see. ___ Oh, I can see Your

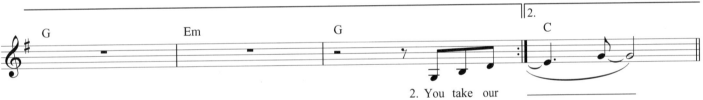
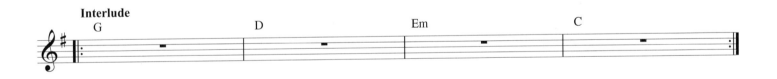
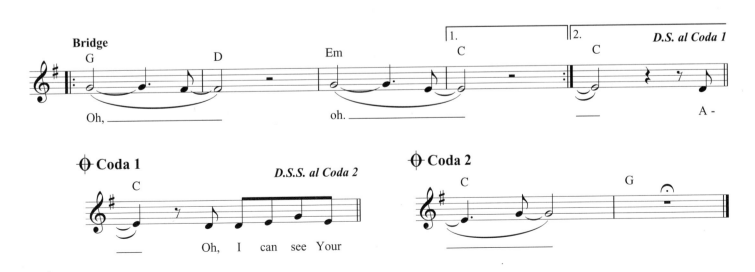

Cornerstone

Words and Music by Jonas Myrin, Reuben Morgan, Eric Liljero and Edward Mote

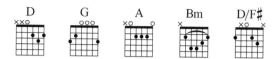

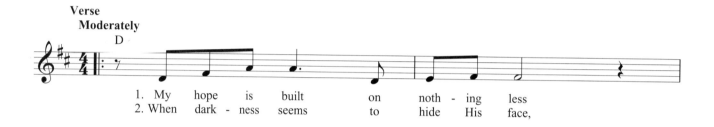

Verse
Moderately

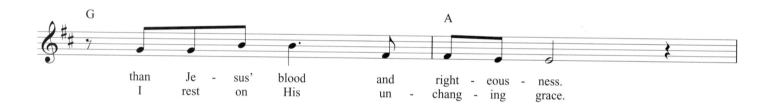

1. My hope is built on noth - ing less
2. When dark - ness seems to hide His face,

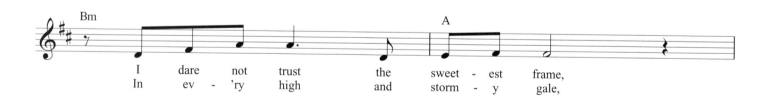

than Je - sus' blood and right - eous - ness.
I rest on His un - chang - ing grace.

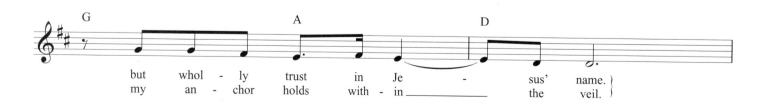

I dare not trust the sweet - est frame,
In ev - 'ry high and storm - y gale,

but whol - ly trust in Je - sus' name. }
my an - chor holds with - in _____ the veil. }

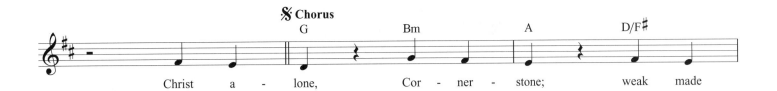

% **Chorus**

Christ a - lone, Cor - ner - stone; weak made

strong in the Sav - ior's love. Through the

To Coda 1.

storm He is Lord, Lord of all.

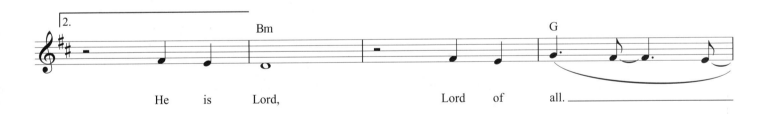

2.

He is Lord, Lord of all. _____

D.S. al Coda   **Coda**

Christ a - Lord of all.

Glorious Day
(Living He Loved Me)

Words and Music by Mark Hall and Michael Bleecker

Additional Lyrics

2. One day they led Him up Calvary's mountain.
   One day they nailed Him to die on a tree.
   Suffering anguish, despised and rejected,
   Bearing our sins, my Redeemer is He.
   The hands that healed nations stretched out on a tree
   And took the nails for me.

3. One day the grave could conceal Him no longer.
   One day the stone rolled away from the door.
   Then He arose; over death He had conquered.
   Now He's ascended, my Lord evermore.
   Death could not hold Him, the grave could not keep Him
   From rising again.

God Is Able

Words and Music by Reuben Morgan and Ben Fielding

Bridge

God is with us, ___ He will

go be - fore. He will nev - er leave us. ___ He will nev - er leave us. ___ God is

for us. ___ He has o - pen ___ arms. He will nev - er fail us. ___ He will nev - er

Chorus

fail us. ___ Lift - ed up, _____ He de-feat - ed the grave. ___ Raised to life, _

___ our God is a - ble. In His Name, ___ we o - ver - come, _

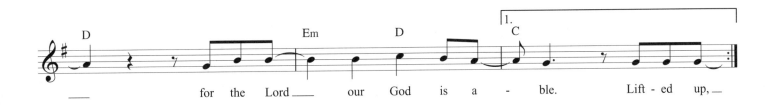

[1.

___ for the Lord ___ our God is a - ble. Lift - ed up, _

Outro

[2.

- ble, for the Lord ___ our God is a - ble, for the Lord _

___ our God is a - ble. _____

Good Good Father

Words and Music by Pat Barrett and Anthony Brown

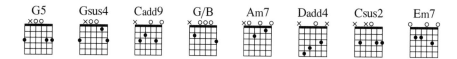

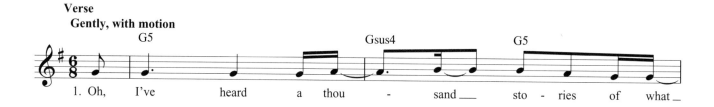

Verse
Gently, with motion

1. Oh, I've heard a thou - sand __ sto - ries of what __

__ they think You're __ like. But I've _____ heard the

ten - der __ whis - per of love __ in the dead of __ night. And You tell __

__ me that You're __ pleased and that I'm _____ nev - er a - lone. __

Chorus

You're a good, _____ good Fa - ther. It's who You are,

it's who You are, it's who You are, _____ and I'm loved __ by

You. It's who I am, __ it's who I am, __ it's who I am. _____

To Coda

Dadd4 ... Verse G5

2. Oh, and I've _____ seen

Gsus4   G5   Gsus4   G5

man - y _____ search - ing for an - swers   far and _____ wide.   But I _____

Gsus4   G5

know   we're   all _____ search - ing   for an - swers   on - ly

Gsus4   G5   Cadd9   G/B

You pro - vide. 'Cause You know _____ just   what   we _____ need   be - fore

D.S. al Coda

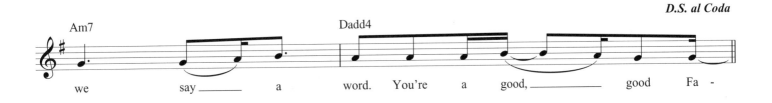

Am7   Dadd4

we   say _____ a   word.   You're   a   good, _____ good   Fa -

Coda

Dadd4   **Bridge** Csus2   Em7

_____ Be-cause You are   per - fect   in   all _____ of   Your ways. _____   You are

Am7   G5   Csus2

per - fect   in   all _____ of   Your ways. _____   You are   per - fect   in   all _____ of   Your ways _____

Em7   Dadd4   1.   2.

_____   to   us.   You are   3. Oh, it's

Verse

love so un-de-ni-a-ble, I, I can hard-ly___ speak.

Peace so un-ex-plain-a-ble, I, I can hard-ly___ think as You call___

___ me deep-er___ still, as You call ___ me deep-er___ still, as You call___

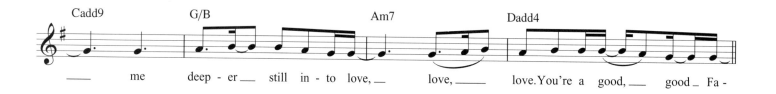

___ me deep-er___ still in-to love, ___ love, _____ love. You're a good, ___ good ___ Fa-

Chorus

- ther. It's who You are, it's who You are, it's who You are, _____

___ and I'm loved___ by You. It's who I am, ___ it's who I am, ___

it's who I am. _____ You're a good, _____ good Fa- ___

Outro

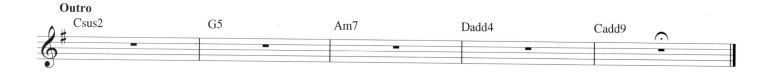

How He Loves

Words and Music by John Mark McMillan

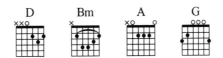

Verse
In a slow 2

He is jeal - ous for me. Loves like a hur - ri - cane;

I am a tree, bend - ing be - neath the weight of His wind and

mer - cy. When all of a sud - den,

I am un - a - ware of these af - flic - tions e - clipsed by glo - ry, and I

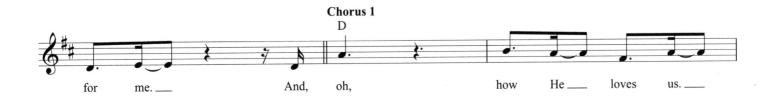

real - ize just how beau - ti - ful You are and how great Your af - fec - tions are

Chorus 1

for me. And, oh, how He loves us.

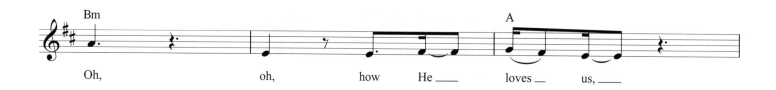

Oh,   oh,   how   He ____ loves ___ us, ____

how   He ____ loves   us _____ all.

Interlude

(Instrumental)

Yeah, He   loves   us.

Oh, ____ how   He   loves   us.   Oh, ____ how   He   loves   us.

Bridge

Oh, ____ how   He   loves. _____ And   we   are   His __ por - tion and

He   is   our __ prize, __ drawn   to   re - demp - tion   by   the   grace   in   His   eyes. __ If   His

grace is an ____ o - cean, ___ we're all ___ sink - ing. ___

And heav - en meets _ earth like an un - fore-seen kiss, and my

heart turns ___ vio - lent-ly in - side of my chest. I don't have __ time to main -

tain these re - grets ___ when I think a - bout the way ___ that He

Chorus 2

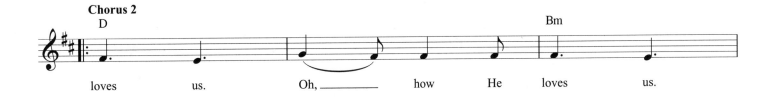

loves us. Oh, _____ how He loves us.

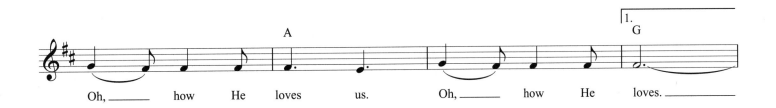

Oh, _____ how He loves us. Oh, _____ how He loves. ___

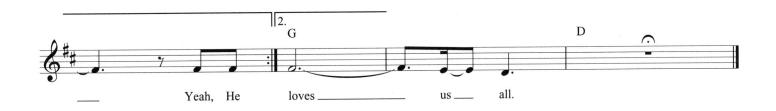

___ Yeah, He loves _____ us __ all.

Great Are You Lord

Words and Music by Jason Ingram, David Leonard and Leslie Jordan

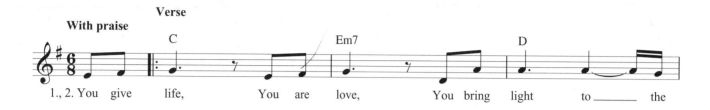

Verse

With praise

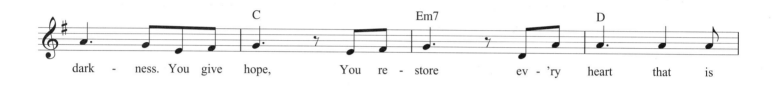

1., 2. You give life, You are love, You bring light to _____ the

dark - ness. You give hope, You re - store ev - 'ry heart that is

bro - ken. And great are You, _____ Lord. _____ It's Your

Chorus

breath in our lungs, so we pour out our praise, we pour out our praise. It's Your

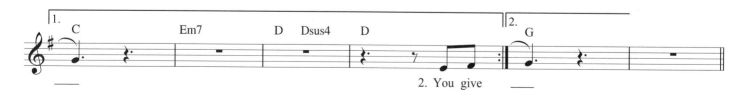

breath in our lungs, so we pour out our praise to You on - ly. _____

1. It's Your ... _____ 2. You give _____

Bridge

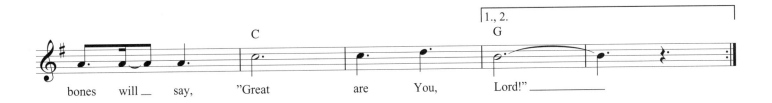

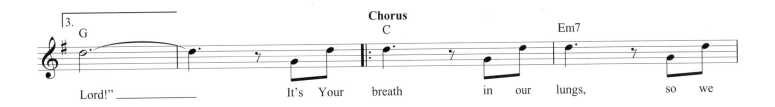

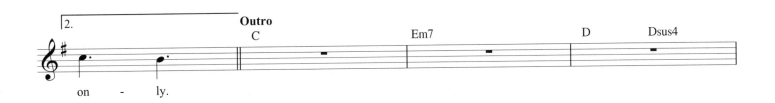

29

Happy Day

Words and Music by Tim Hughes and Ben Cantellon

my sin a - way. Oh, hap - py day, ___ hap - py day, ___ I'll nev -

- er be the same. ___ For - ev -

To Coda ⊕

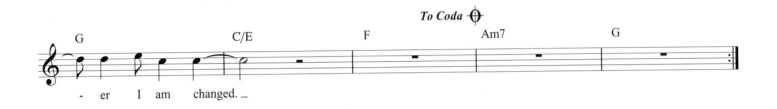

- er I am changed. _

Bridge

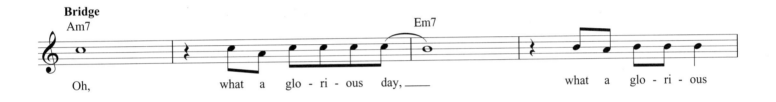

Oh, what a glo - ri - ous day, ___ what a glo - ri - ous

way that You have ___ saved ___ me. And, oh, ___

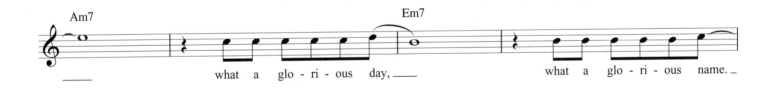

___ what a glo - ri - ous day, ___ what a glo - ri - ous name. _

D.S. al Coda

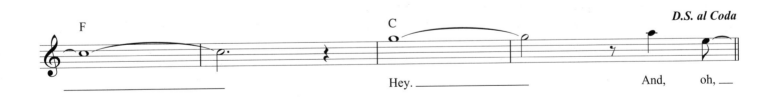

Hey. ___ And, oh, ___

⊕ **Coda**   **Outro**

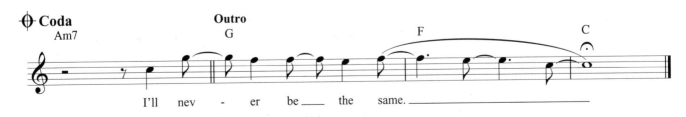

I'll nev - er be ___ the same. ___

Holy Spirit

Words and Music by Katie Torwalt and Bryan Torwalt

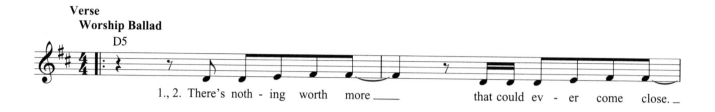

Verse
Worship Ballad

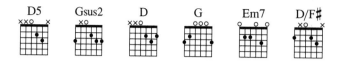

1., 2. There's noth - ing worth more _____ that could ev - er come close. _

_____ No thing can com - pare; _____ You're our liv - ing hope. _____

Your pres - ence, _____ Lord. I've tast - ed and seen _

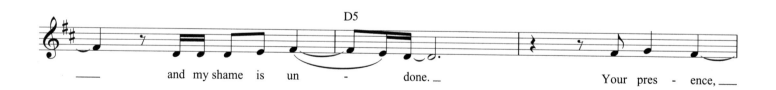

_____ of the sweet - est of loves, _____ where my heart be - comes free _____

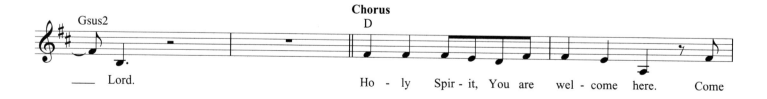

_____ and my shame is un - done. _ Your pres - ence, _____

Chorus

_____ Lord. Ho - ly Spir - it, You are wel - come here. Come

flood this place and fill the at - mos - phere. Your glo - ry, God, is what our

hearts long for, to be o - ver - come by Your pres - ence, Lord. ____

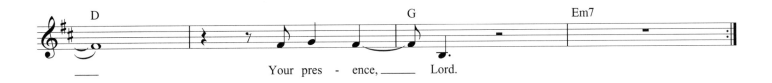

Your pres - ence, ____ Lord.

Bridge

Let us ____ be - come ____ more a - ware ____ of Your pres - ence. ____

Play 4 times

Let us ____ ex - pe - ri - ence ____ the glo - ry of ____ Your good - ness. ____

Ho - ly Spir - it, You are wel - come here. Come

flood this place and fill the at - mos - phere. Your glo - ry, God, is what our

hearts long for, to be o - ver - come by Your pres - ence, Lord. ____

Hosanna
(Praise Is Rising)

Words and Music by Paul Baloche and Brenton Brown

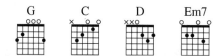

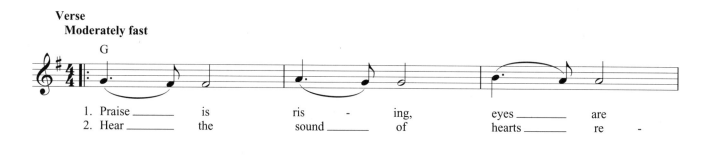

Verse
Moderately fast

1. Praise _____ is ris - ing, eyes _____ are
2. Hear _____ the sound _____ of hearts _____ re -

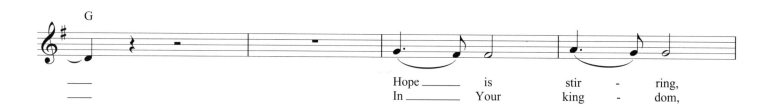

turn - ing _____ to You. _____ We turn to You. _____
turn - ing _____ to You. _____ We turn to You. _____

_____ Hope _____ is stir - ring,
_____ In _____ Your king - dom,

hearts _____ are yearn - ing _____ for You. _____
bro - ken lives are _____ made new. _____

We long for You. _____
You make us new. _____

'Cause when we see _____

Pre-Chorus

_____ You, we find strength _____ to face the day.

In Your pres - ence, all our fears ____ are washed a - way,

washed a - way. ____ Ho - san -

na, ho - san - na. ____ You are the God ____

____ who saves us, ____ wor - thy of all ____ our prais - es. ____

____ Ho - san - na, ho - san - na. ____

____ Come have Your way ____ a - mong us. ____ We wel - come You here, ____

____ Lord Je - sus. ____

Great I Am

Words and Music by Jared Anderson

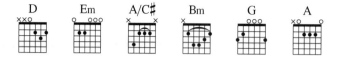

Verse
Moderate Pop beat

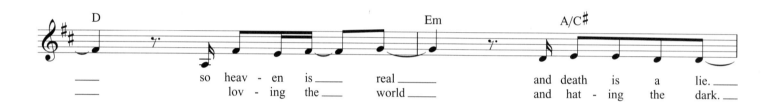

1. I wan-na be ___ close, ___ close to Your side, ___
2. I wan-na be ___ near, ___ near to Your heart, ___

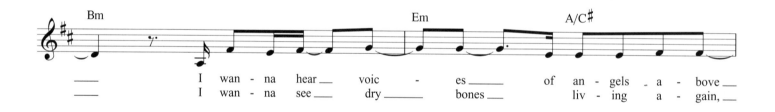

___ so heav-en is ___ real ___ and death is a lie. ___
___ lov - ing the ___ world ___ and hat-ing the dark. ___

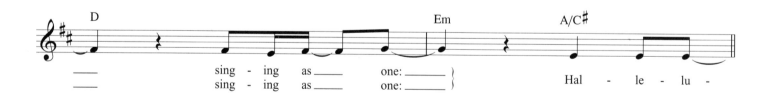

___ I wan-na hear ___ voic - es ___ of an-gels _ a - bove ___
___ I wan-na see ___ dry ___ bones ___ liv-ing a - gain, ___

___ sing - ing as ___ one: ___
___ sing - ing as ___ one: ___   Hal - le - lu -

Chorus

- jah! Ho - ly, ho - ly! God Al-might - y, the great I ___ AM. ___

Who is wor - thy? None be - side _____ Thee, God Al - might-

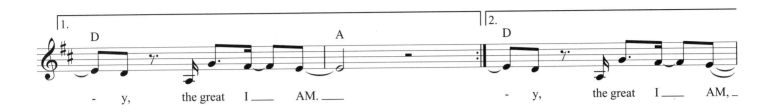

1.
- y, the great I _____ AM. _____

2.
- y, the great I _____ AM, _

_____ the great I _____ AM. _____

Bridge

The moun - tains shake be - fore You, the de - mons run and flee

at the men - tion of the name King of Maj - es - ty.

There is no pow'r in hell or an - y who can stand

be - fore the pow - er and the pres - ence of the great I _____ AM, _____

_the great I___ AM, _____ the great I___ AM. _____ Yeah, _____

Chorus

yeah. Hal - le - lu - jah! Ho - ly, ho - ly! God Al - might -

- y, the great I___ AM. ___ Who is wor - thy? None be - side _

1.

___ Thee, God Al - might - y, the great I___ AM. ___ Hal - le - lu -

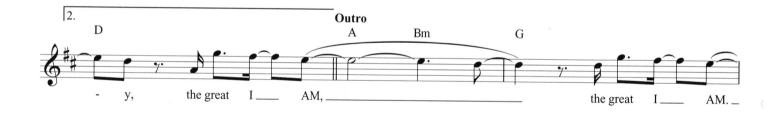

2.   **Outro**

- y, the great I___ AM, _____ the great I___ AM. _

_____ He's the great I___ AM, _____

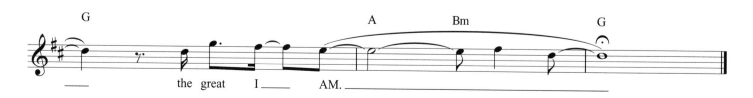

___ the great I___ AM. _____

38

We Believe

Words and Music by Travis Ryan, Matthew Hooper and Richie Fike

Verse
Moderately slow, in 2

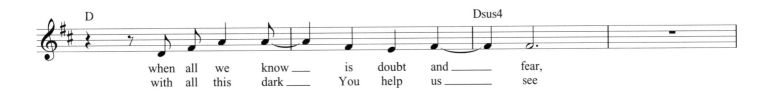

1. In this time ___ of des - per - a - tion,
2. In this bro - ken gen - er - a - tion,

when all we know ___ is doubt and ___ fear,
with all this dark ___ You help us ___ see

there is on - ly one ___ foun - da - tion; ___
there is on - ly one ___ sal - va - tion; ___
we be - lieve, ___

1.
2.

we be - lieve. ___
We be - lieve ___

Chorus

___ in God the Fa - ther, we be - lieve ___ in Je - sus Christ, ___

___ we be - lieve ___ in the Ho - ly Spir - it, and He's

giv - en us ___ new life. ___ We be - lieve ___ in the cru - ci - fix -

- ion, we be - lieve ___ that He con-quered death, ___ we be - lieve ___

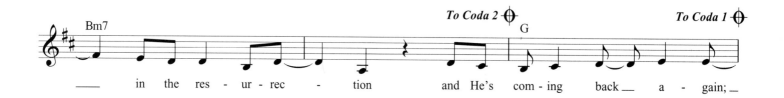

___ in the res - ur - rec - tion and He's com - ing back ___ a - gain; ___

___ we be - lieve. ___ 3. So,

Verse

let our faith ___ be more ___ than an - thems, ___

great - er than ___ the songs ___ we ___ sing.

And in our weak - ness and ___ temp - ta - tions, ___

we be - lieve, ___ we be - lieve. ___

Jesus Messiah

Words and Music by Chris Tomlin, Jesse Reeves, Daniel Carson and Ed Cash

Additional Lyrics

2. His body the bread, His blood the wine,
Broken and poured out, all for love.
The whole earth trembled and the veil was torn.
Love so amazing, love so amazing.

Lead Me to the Cross

Words and Music by Brooke Ligertwood

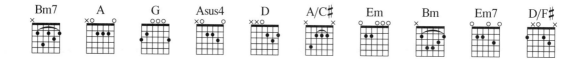

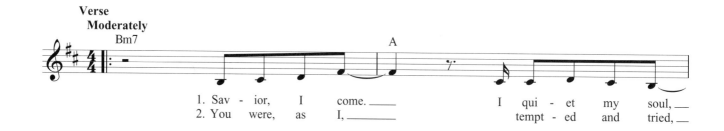

Verse
Moderately

1. Sav - ior, I come. ___ I qui - et my soul, ___
2. You were, as I, ___ tempt - ed and tried, ___

re - mem - ber ___ re - demp - tion's hill ___
hu - man. ___ Word be - came flesh, ___

where Your blood was spilled ___ for my ran - som. ___
bore my sin and death. ___ Now You're ris - en. ___

Pre-Chorus

And ev - 'ry - thing ___ I once ___ held dear, ___ I count ___

___ it all ___ as loss. ___ Lead me to the cross ___ where Your love poured _ out. _

Bring me to my knees. _ Lord, I lay me _ down. _ Rid me of _ my - self,

I be - long to ___ You. ___ Oh, lead me, ___

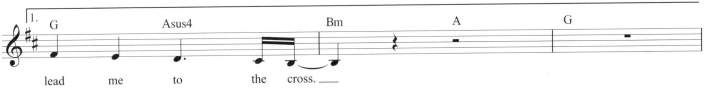

1. lead me to the cross. ___

2. lead me to Your

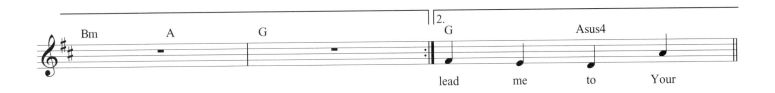

Bridge

heart. _____ Lead me to ___ Your

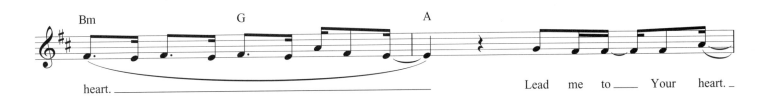

heart. _____ Lead me to ___ Your

heart. _____ Lead me to ___ Your heart. ___

D.S. al Coda

Lead me to the cross _

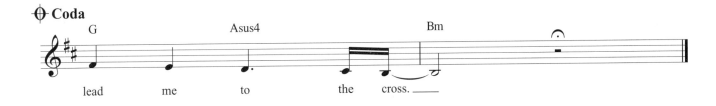

⊕ **Coda**

lead me to the cross. ___

Oceans
(Where Feet May Fail)

Words and Music by Joel Houston, Matt Crocker and Salomon Lighthelm

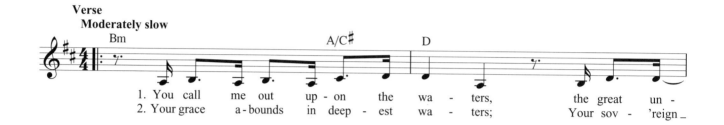

Verse
Moderately slow

1. You call me out up-on the wa-ters, the great un-
2. Your grace a-bounds in deep-est wa-ters; Your sov - 'reign

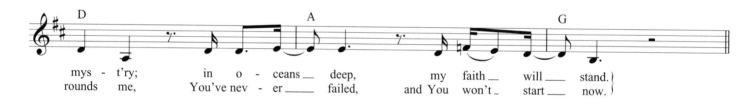

- known where feet may __ fail. And there I find You in the
___ hand will be my __ guide. Where feet may fail and fear sur-

mys - t'ry; in o - ceans __ deep, my faith __ will __ stand.
rounds me, You've nev - er __ failed, and You won't __ start __ now.

Chorus

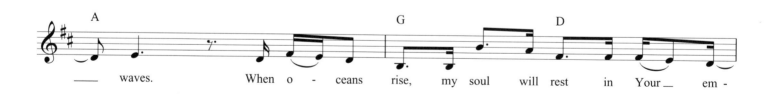

And I will call up-on __ Your __ name and keep my eyes a - bove __ the __

___ waves. When o - ceans rise, my soul will rest in Your __ em -

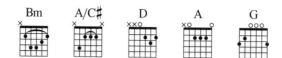

- brace, __ for I am Yours, You are __ mine.

Bridge

Spir - it, lead ___ me where ___ my trust ___

___ is with - out bor - ders. Let me walk ___ up - on ___ the wa - ters, wher-ev -

- er You ___ would call me. Take me deep - er than ___ my feet ___

___ could ev - er wan - der, and my faith ___ will be ___ made strong - er in the pres-

Outro-Chorus

- ence of ___ my Sav - ior. I will call up - on ___ Your ___ name.

Keep my eyes a - bove ___ the ___ waves. My soul will rest in Your ___ em-

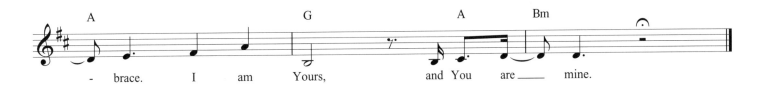

- brace. I am Yours, and You are ___ mine.

Open Up the Heavens

Words and Music by Jason Ingram, Stuart Garrard, Andi Rozier, James MacDonald and Meredith Andrews

Our God

Words and Music by Jonas Myrin, Chris Tomlin, Matt Redman and Jesse Reeves

Revelation Song

Words and Music by Jennie Lee Riddle

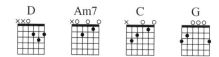

This Is Amazing Grace

Words and Music by Phil Wickham, Joshua Neil Farro and Jeremy Riddle

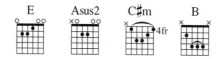

Verse
Moderate Rock beat

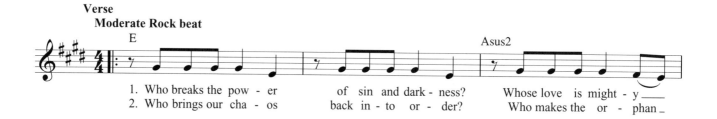

1. Who breaks the pow - er of sin and dark - ness? Whose love is might - y ___
2. Who brings our cha - os back in - to or - der? Who makes the or - phan _

and so much strong - er? ___ The King of glo - ry, the King a - bove all ___ kings. _
a son and daugh - ter? ___ The King of glo - ry,

Play 1st time only

Play 2nd time only

___ the King of glo - ry. Who shakes the whole earth
Who rules the na - tions

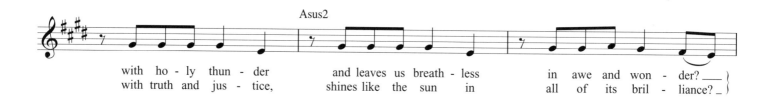

with ho - ly thun - der and leaves us breath - less in awe and won - der? ___
with truth and jus - tice, shines like the sun in all of its bril - liance? _

The King of glo - ry, the King a - bove all ___ kings. _ This is a - maz - ing _ grace, _

____ this is un - fail - ing __ love, _____

that You would take my __ place, __ that You would bear my __ cross. __

____ You __ laid down Your _ life _____

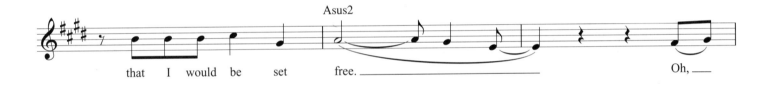

that I would be set free. _____ Oh, ___

To Coda ⊕

Je - sus, I sing __ for all that You've done for __ me. ___

Bridge

Wor - thy is the Lamb who was slain. __ Wor - thy is the King who con -

- quered the grave. _ Wor - thy is the Lamb who was slain. ___

Asus2

Wor - thy is the King who con - quered the grave. _ Wor - thy is the Lamb who was slain. _

Asus2

_ Wor - thy is the King who con - quered the grave. _

C#m   E   Asus2

Wor - thy is the Lamb who was slain. __ Wor - thy, wor - thy, wor - thy! _ Oh, _

Coda

D.S. al Coda

Outro

B   E

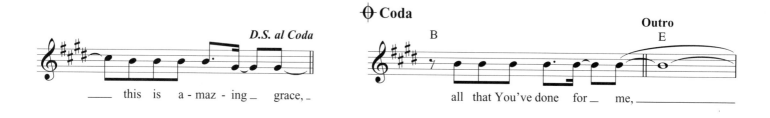

___ this is a - maz - ing _ grace, _   all that You've done for _ me, _____

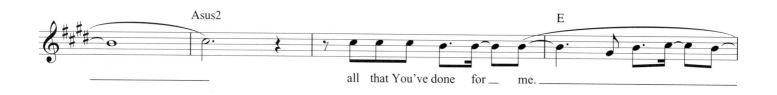

Asus2   E

_____ all that You've done for _ me. _____

Asus2   E

_____

Whom Shall I Fear
(God of Angel Armies)

Words and Music by Chris Tomlin, Ed Cash and Scott Cash

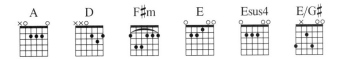

Verse
Moderately

1. You hear me when I call, You are my morn - ing song.

Though dark - ness fills the night, it can - not hide the light. _____

Whom shall ___ I _____ fear?

Verse

2. You crush the en - e - my   un - der - neath my feet.
3. My strength is in Your name,   for You a - lone can save.

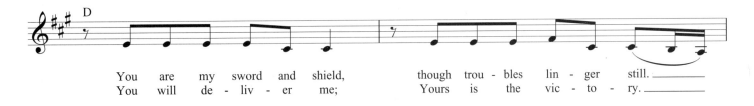

You are my sword and shield,   though trou - bles lin - ger still. _____
You will de - liv - er me;   Yours is the vic - to - ry. _____

Whom shall ___ I _____ fear?
Whom shall ___ I _____ fear?

𝄋 Chorus

I know who goes be - fore me, I know who stands be - hind.

The God of an - gel ar - mies is al - ways by my side.

The One who reigns for - ev - er, He is a friend of mine.

To Coda ⊕

The God of an - gel ar - mies is al - ways by my

side. side. And

Bridge

noth - ing formed a - gainst me ___ shall ___ stand. ___

You hold the whole ___ world in Your ___ hands. ___

I'm hold - ing on ___ to Your prom - is - es; ___ You are

faith - ful, ___ You are faith - ful. ___ And faith - ful, ___ You are

faith - ful, ___ You are faith - ful. ___

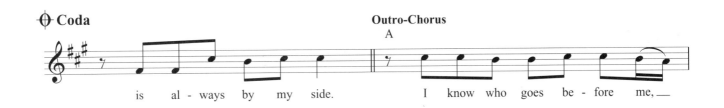

Coda **Outro-Chorus**

is al - ways by my side. I know who goes be - fore me, ___

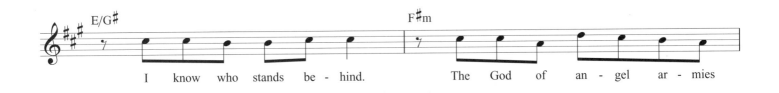

I know who stands be - hind. The God of an - gel ar - mies

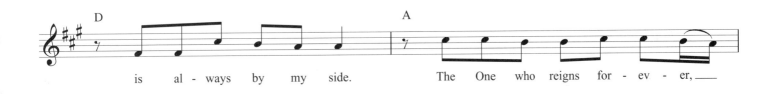

is al - ways by my side. The One who reigns for - ev - er, ___

He is a friend of mine. The God of an - gel ar - mies

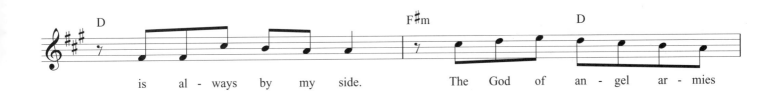

is al - ways by my side. The God of an - gel ar - mies

is al - ways by my side.

Your Grace Is Enough

Words and Music by Matt Maher

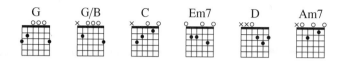

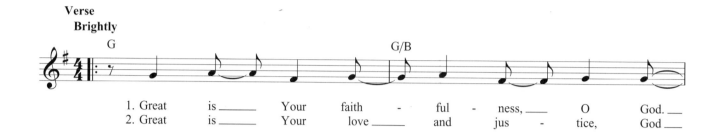

1. Great   is ____ Your   faith - ful - ness, ____ O   God. ____
2. Great   is ____ Your   love ____ and   jus - tice,   God ____

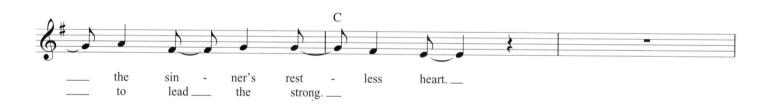

____ of   Ja - cob.   You   wres - tle   with ____
____ to   lead ____ the   strong. ____ You   use ____ the   weak ____

the   sin - ner's   rest - less   heart. ____
to   lead ____ the   strong. ____

You   lead ____ us   by ____ still   wa - ters   in -
You   lead ____ us   in ____ the   song ____ of   Your ____

- to   mer - cy,   and   noth - ing   can ____
____ sal - va - tion,   and   all ____ Your   peo -

_____ keep us _____ a - part. _____
- ple sing _____ a - long. _____

So re -

Pre-Chorus

Am7   G/B   C

mem - ber _____ Your peo - ple, _____ re - mem - ber _____ Your

D   Em7   D   G/B

chil - dren, _____ re - mem - ber _____ Your prom - ise, O God. _____

Chorus

C   G

_____ Your grace is e - nough, _

D   Em7   C

_____ Your grace is e - nough, _____ Your

To Coda

G   D   C

grace is e - nough _____ for _____ me. _____

1.   **2.** *D.S. al Coda*   **Coda**

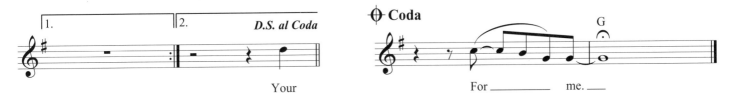

Your   G

For _____ me. _____

christianguitarsongbooks

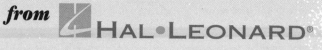

from

ACOUSTIC GUITAR WORSHIP

30 praise song favorites arranged for guitar, including: Awesome God • Forever • I Could Sing of Your Love Forever • Lord, Reign in Me • Open the Eyes of My Heart • and more.
00699672 Solo Guitar...$9.95

FAVORITE HYMNS FOR EASY GUITAR

48 hymns, including: All Hail the Power of Jesus' Name • Amazing Grace • Be Thou My Vision • Blessed Assurance • Fairest Lord Jesus • I Love to Tell the Story • In the Garden • Let Us Break Bread Together • Rock of Ages • Were You There? • When I Survey the Wondrous Cross • and more.
00702041 Easy Guitar with Notes & Tab $9.95

GOSPEL FAVORITES FOR GUITAR

An amazing collection of 49 favorites, including: Amazing Grace • Did You Stop to Pray This Morning • How Great Thou Art • The King Is Coming • My God Is Real • Nearer, My God to Thee • The Old Rugged Cross • Precious Lord, Take My Hand • Will the Circle Be Unbroken • and more.
00699374 Easy Guitar with Notes & Tab $14.95

GOSPEL GUITAR SONGBOOK

Includes notes & tab for fingerpicking and Travis picking arrangements of 15 favorites: Amazing Grace • Blessed Assurance • Do Lord • I've Got Peace Like a River • Just a Closer Walk with Thee • O Happy Day • Precious Memories • Rock of Ages • Swing Low, Sweet Chariot • There Is Power in the Blood • When the Saints Go Marching In • and more!
00695372 Guitar with Notes & Tab $9.95

THE GOSPEL SONGS BOOK

A virtual bible of more than 100 songs of faith arranged for easy guitar! This collection includes: Amazing Grace • Blessed Assurance • Church in the Wildwood • His Eye Is on the Sparrow • I Love to Tell the Story • Just a Closer Walk with Thee • The Lily of the Valley • More Than Wonderful • The Old Rugged Cross • Rock of Ages • Shall We Gather at the River? • Turn Your Radio On • Will the Circle Be Unbroken • and more.
00702157 Easy Guitar.....................................$15.95

GREATEST HYMNS FOR GUITAR

48 hymns, including: Abide with Me • Amazing Grace • Be Still My Soul • Glory to His Name • In the Garden • and more.
00702116 Easy Guitar with Notes & Tab $8.95

BEST OF HILLSONG UNITED

Easy arrangements with notes & tab for 18 great hits from Hillsong United. Includes: All I Need Is You • Came to My Rescue • From the Inside Out • Hosanna • Lead Me to the Cross • The Stand • Take It All • and more!
00702288 Easy Guitar..$12.99

THE HYMN BOOK

143 glorious hymns: Abide with Me • Be Thou My Vision • Come, Thou Fount of Every Blessing • Fairest Lord Jesus • Holy, Holy, Holy • Just a Closer Walk with Thee • Nearer, My God, to Thee • Rock of Ages • more. Perfect for church services, sing-alongs, bible camps and more!
00702142 Easy Guitar (no tab) $14.99

PRAISE AND WORSHIP FOR GUITAR

45 easy arrangements, including: As the Deer • Glorify Thy Name • He Is Exalted • Holy Ground • How Excellent Is Thy Name • Majesty • Thou Art Worthy • You Are My Hiding Place • more.
00702125 Easy Guitar with Notes & Tab $9.95

PRAISE & WORSHIP – STRUM & SING

This inspirational collection features 25 favorites for guitarists to strum and sing. Includes chords and lyrics for: Amazing Grace (My Chains Are Gone) • Cornerstone • Everlasting God • Forever • The Heart of Worship • How Great Is Our God • In Christ Alone • Mighty to Save • 10,000 Reasons (Bless the Lord) • This I Believe • We Fall Down • and more.
00152381 Guitar/Vocal...$12.99

RELIENT K – MMHMM

14 transcriptions from the 2004 release by these Christian punk rockers. Features: Be My Escape • Let It All Out • Life After Death and Taxes • My Girl's Ex-Boyfriend • The One I'm Waiting For • When I Go Down • Which to Bury; Us or the Hatchet? • Who I Am Hates Who I've Been • and more.
00690779 Guitar Recorded Versions $19.95

SWITCHFOOT – THE BEAUTIFUL LETDOWN

All 11 songs in transcriptions with tab from the 2003 release by these Dove Award-winning alt CCM rockers: Adding to the Noise • Ammunition • Beautiful Letdown • Dare You to Move • Gone • Meant to Live • More Than Fine • On Fire • Redemption • This Is Your Life • 24.
00690767 Guitar Recorded Versions $19.95

TOP CHRISTIAN HITS

14 of today's hottest CCM hits: Blessed Be Your Name (Tree 63) • Dare You to Move (Switchfoot) • Filled with Your Glory (Starfield) • Gone (TOBYMAC) • Holy (Nichole Nordeman) • Holy Is the Lord (Chris Tomlin) • I Can Only Imagine (MercyMe) • Much of You (Steven Curtis Chapman) • and more.
00702217 Easy Guitar with Notes & Tab $12.95

THE WORSHIP BOOK

Easy arrangements (no tab) of 80 great worship tunes, including: Above All • Days of Elijah • Forever • Here I Am to Worship • Mighty to Save • Open the Eyes of My Heart • Shout to the Lord • Sing to the King • We Fall Down • and more.
00702247 Easy Guitar.....................................$14.99

TOP WORSHIP HITS

30 songs: Beautiful One • Blessed Be Your Name • God of Wonders • Hosanna (Praise Is Rising) • I Give You My Heart • Mighty to Save • Revelation Song • Sing to the King • Your Grace Is Enough • and more.
00702294 Easy Guitar with Notes & Tab $14.99

THE WORSHIP GUITAR ANTHOLOGY – VOLUME 1

This collection contains melody, lyrics & chords for 100 contemporary favorites, such as: Beautiful One • Forever • Here I Am to Worship • Hosanna (Praise Is Rising) • How He Loves • In Christ Alone • Mighty to Save • Our God • Revelation Song • Your Grace Is Enough • and dozens more.
00101864 Melody/Lyrics/Chords...........................$16.99

Prices, contents and availability subject to change without notice.

FOR MORE INFORMATION, SEE YOUR LOCAL MUSIC DEALER, OR WRITE TO:

HAL•LEONARD®
C O R P O R A T I O N
7777 W. BLUEMOUND RD. P.O. BOX 13819 MILWAUKEE, WI 53213

www.halleonard.com

▶ praisecharts from HAL LEONARD

The PraiseCharts series features volumes of six compatible books that can be used alone or in any combination. The arrangements are designed to aid the flow of live congregational worship, and the level is suitable for amateurs and pros alike. Section numbers and lyric cues are included in each book so musicians can play together easily. Use the downloadable audio tracks in lieu of a live band, or to enhance the sound of your band for rehearsal and performance.

▶ praisecharts — Worship Band Edition

Contemporary Worship Classics
10 Powerful Songs with Audio Access

Features:
• Lead Sheets (3-Part Vocal)
• Chord Charts
• Rhythm Charts
• Online Audio

HAL•LEONARD®

▶ praisecharts — Worship Band Edition

Christmas Praise Carols
10 Contemporary Arrangements with Audio Access

Features:
• Lead Sheets (3-Part Vocal)
• Chord Charts
• Rhythm Charts
• Online Audio Tracks

HAL•LEONARD®

CONTEMPORARY WORSHIP CLASSICS

Book/Online Audio

Amazing Grace (My Chains Are Gone) • Blessed Be Your Name • Forever • God of Wonders • Here I Am to Worship (Light of the World) • Holy Is the Lord • In Christ Alone • Mighty to Save • Sing to the King • Your Name.

00149722	Piano/Vocal + Chord Charts	$16.99
00149723	Worship Band Edition	$14.99
00149724	C Instruments (Treble Clef)	$14.99
00149725	C Instruments (Bass Clef)	$14.99
00149726	B♭ Instruments	$14.99
00149727	E♭ Instruments	$14.99

CHRISTMAS PRAISE CAROLS

Book/Online Audio

Angels We Have Heard on High • Come, Thou Long-Expected Jesus • The First Noel • Go, Tell It on the Mountain • It Came upon the Midnight Clear • Joy to the World • O Come, All Ye Faithful • O Little Town of Bethlehem • Silent Night • What Child Is This.

00149368	Piano/Vocal + Chord Charts	$16.99
00149369	Worship Band Edition	$14.99
00149370	C Instruments (Treble Clef)	$14.99
00149371	C Instruments (Bass Clef)	$14.99
00149372	B♭ Instruments	$14.99
00149373	E♭ Instruments	$14.99

Prices, content and availability subject to change without notice.

HAL•LEONARD®
CORPORATION
7777 W. BLUEMOUND RD. P.O. BOX 13819 MILWAUKEE, WI 53213

www.halleonard.com

Worship Band Play-Along

The **Worship Band Play-Along** series is a flexible tool for worship leaders and bands. Each volume offers five separate, correlated book/CD packs: Guitar, Keyboard, Bass, Drumset, and Vocal. Bands can use the printed music and chord charts to play live together, and members can rehearse at home with the CD tracks. Worship leaders without a band can play/sing along with the CD for a fuller sound. The eight songs in each volume follow a similar theme for easy set selection, and the straightforward arrangements are perfect for bands of any level.

1. Holy Is the Lord

Includes: Agnus Dei • Be Unto Your Name • God of Wonders • Holy Is the Lord • It Is You • Open the Eyes of My Heart • We Fall Down • You Are Holy (Prince of Peace).

08740302	Vocal	$12.95
08740333	Keyboard	$12.95
08740334	Guitar	$12.95
08740335	Bass	$12.95
08740336	Drumset	$12.95

2. Here I Am to Worship

Includes: Come, Now Is the Time to Worship • Give Us Clean Hands • Hear Our Praises • Here I Am to Worship • I Give You My Heart • Let Everything That Has Breath • You Alone • You're Worthy of My Praise.

08740337	Vocal	$12.95
08740338	Keyboard	$12.95
08740409	Guitar	$12.95
08740441	Bass	$12.95
08740444	Drumset	$12.95

3. How Great Is Our God

Includes: Above All • Beautiful Savior (All My Days) • Days of Elijah • How Great Is Our God • Let My Words Be Few (I'll Stand in Awe of You) • No One Like You • Wonderful Maker • Yesterday, Today and Forever.

08740540	Vocal	$12.95
08740571	Keyboard	$12.95
08740572	Guitar	$12.95
08740608	Bass	$12.95
08740635	Drumset	$12.95

4. He Is Exalted

Includes: Beautiful One • God of All • He Is Exalted • In Christ Alone • Lord Most High • Lord, Reign in Me • We Want to See Jesus Lifted High • Worthy Is the Lamb.

08740646	Vocal	$12.99
08740651	Keyboard	$12.99
08740712	Guitar	$12.99
08740741	Bass	$12.99
08745665	Drumset	$12.99

5. Joy to the World

Angels We Have Heard on High • Away in a Manger • Hark! the Herald Angels Sing • Joy to the World • O Come, All Ye Faithful (Adeste Fideles) • O Come, O Come, Emmanuel • Silent Night • What Child Is This?.

08749919	Vocal	$12.99
08749921	Guitar	$12.99
08749923	Drumset	$12.99

FOR MORE INFORMATION, SEE YOUR LOCAL MUSIC DEALER, OR WRITE TO:

HAL•LEONARD®
C O R P O R A T I O N
7777 W. BLUEMOUND RD. P.O. BOX 13819 MILWAUKEE, WI 53213

www.halleonard.com

Prices, contents, and availability subject to change without notice.

0815